Patterns in the
CITY

by J. Clark Sawyer

Consultant: Kimberly Brenneman, PhD
National Institute for Early Education Research, Rutgers University
New Brunswick, New Jersey

BEARPORT
PUBLISHING

New York, New York

Credits

Cover, © Action Sports Photography/Shutterstock; TOC, © Nancy Louie/Getty Images; 4–5, © Ocean/Corbis; 6–7, © Denis Belyaevskiy/Thinkstock; 6, © Sean Pavone/Shutterstock; 8–9, © Giovanni Rinaldi/Thinkstock; 10–11, © Keith Levit/Thinkstock; 12–13, © Andria Patino/Corbis; 14–15, © Max Topchii/Shutterstock; 16–17, © pryzmat/Shutterstock; 18–19, © Colin/Wikimedia Commons; 20–21, © Rafael Elias/Getty Images; 22–23, © Nancy Louie/Getty Images; 24–25, © daizuoxin/Thinkstock; 26–27, © age fotostock/Alamy; 28–29, © Jeff Badger/Alamy; 30A, © Hugh Williamson/Alamy; 30B, © FlavoredPixels/Thinkstock; 30C, © hakiagena/Alamy; 30D, © Henrik Sorensen/Getty Images; 31TL, © Keith Levit/Thinkstock; 31TM, © Feng Yu/Shutterstock; 31TR, © darloboy/Thinkstock; 31BL, © qingwa/Thinkstock; 31BM, © nailiaschwarz/Thinkstock; 31BR, © Isaak/Shutterstock.

Publisher: Kenn Goin
Editor: Jessica Rudolph
Creative Director: Spencer Brinker
Design: Debrah Kaiser
Photo Researcher: Michael Win

Library of Congress Cataloging-in-Publication Data

Clark Sawyer, J., author.
  Patterns in the city / by J. Clark Sawyer.
     pages cm. — (Seeing Patterns All Around)
  Includes bibliographical references and index.
  ISBN-13: 978-1-62724-336-0 (library binding)
  ISBN-10: 1-62724-336-4 (library binding)
  1. Pattern perception—Juvenile literature. 2. Shapes—Juvenile literature. 3. Cities and towns—Juvenile literature. I. Title.
  BF294.C53 2015
  516.15—dc23
                                    2014008473

For more information, write to Bearport Publishing Company, Inc., 45 West 21st Street, Suite 3B, New York, New York 10010. Printed in the United States of America.

10 9 8 7 6 5 4 3 2 1

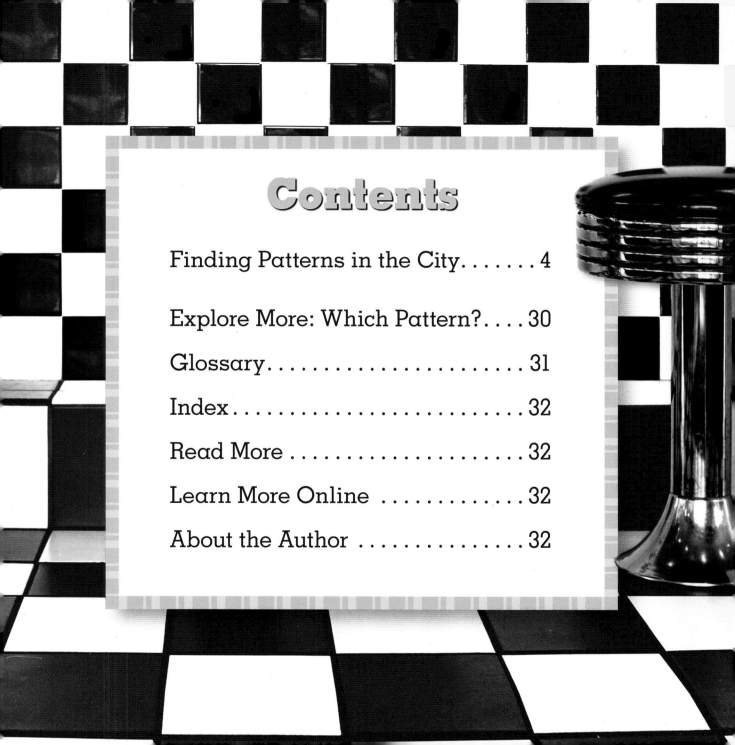

Contents

Finding Patterns in the City

Patterns can be shapes, colors, or sizes that repeat.

You can see patterns all around a city.

White lines in a crosswalk make a striped pattern.

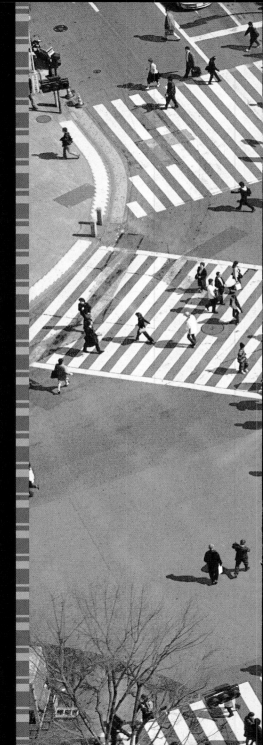

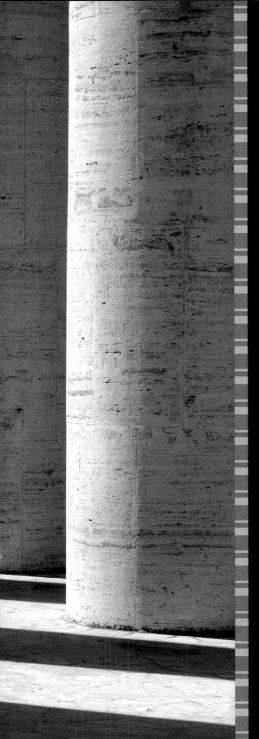

A row of **columns** makes a pattern.

The shadows of the columns make a pattern, too.

7

Pigeons sit on a fence.

Gray, white.

8

The colors repeat.

They make an **alternating** pattern.

The seats on a **subway** make a colorful pattern.

Orange, orange, yellow, yellow.

The pattern goes on and on.

11

A family makes
a pattern.

Short, tall.

This pattern repeats.

13

Lights in the windows of a building make a pattern.

On, off.

The pattern repeats over and over.

15

Patterns can go round and round!

This staircase has a **spiral** pattern.

17

Dogs can have spotted patterns.

The spots are different shapes and sizes.

This is an **irregular pattern**.

19

Rows of buttons in an elevator make a pattern of circles.

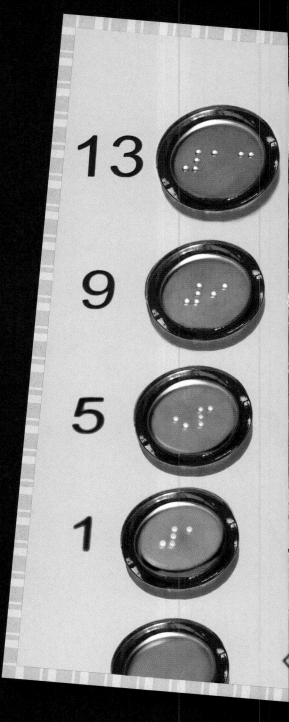

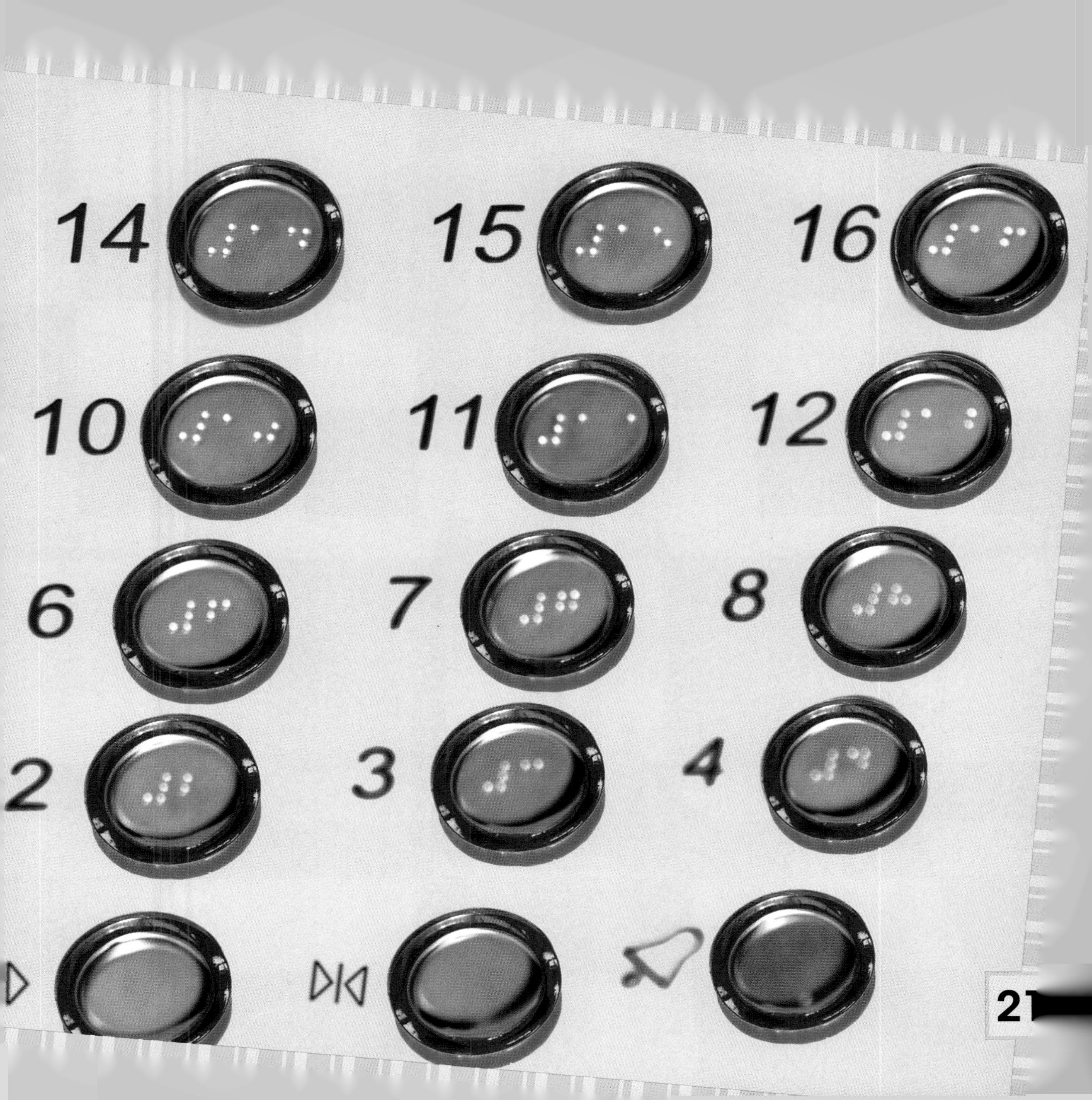
14
15
16
10
11
12
6
7
8
2
3
4

Square tiles make a **checkerboard** pattern.

The squares are two different colors.

23

Some patterns
include many
different shapes.

What shapes do you
see in this fence?

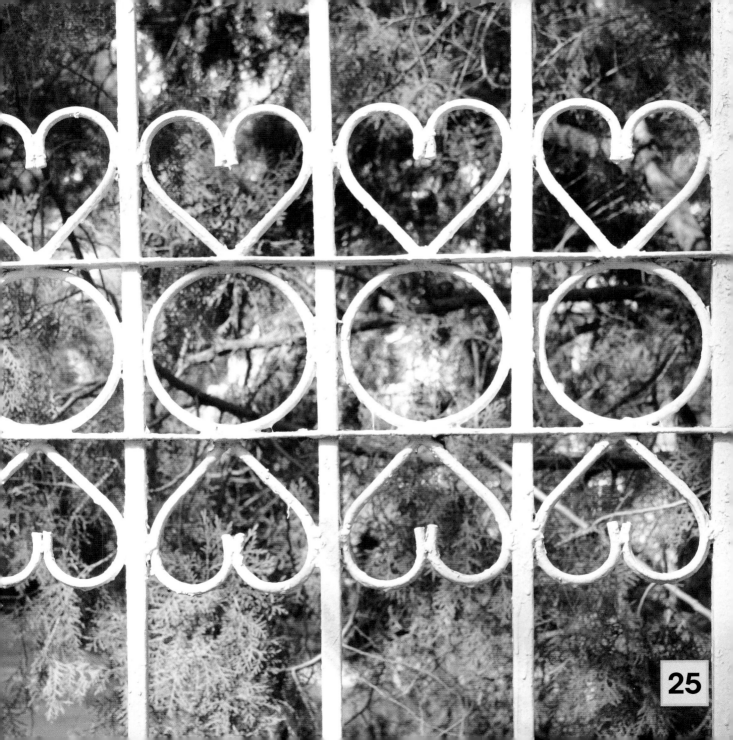

25

Patterns can be small.

Flowers in a park have a pattern.

The purple and yellow colors repeat on every petal.

Patterns can also be huge.

From an airplane, city streets look like giant rectangles.

Look around and you'll see patterns everywhere!

Explore More:
Which Pattern?

Look at the pictures below. Each one shows a kind of pattern that can be found in a city. Match each pattern with the correct picture.

A
B
C
D

1. spiral pattern

3. striped pattern

2. irregular pattern

4. checkerboard pattern

Answers are on page 32.

Glossary

alternating
(AWL-tur-*nayt*-ing)
changing back and
forth, such as between
two colors

checkerboard
(CHEK-ur-bord)
a design that shows
squares in two
alternating colors

columns (KOL-uhmz)
tall upright supports for
a building

irregular pattern
(ih-REG-yuh-lur PAT-
urn) a pattern that has
one or more similar
parts unequal in size,
shape, or in the way
they are arranged

spiral (SPYE-ruhl)
winding or circling
around a center

subway (SUHB-way)
an electric train that
runs underground
in a city

Index

Read More

Olson, Nathan. *City Patterns.*
North Mankato, MN: Capstone
(2007).

Pluckrose, Henry. *Pattern
(Math Counts).* Chicago:
Children's Press (1995).

Learn More Online

To learn more about city patterns, visit
www.bearportpublishing.com/SeeingPatternsAllAround

About the Author

J. Clark Sawyer lives in Connecticut. She has
edited and written many books about history,
science, and nature for children.

Answers for Page 30:

1. B; 2. C; 3. A; 4. D

32